I0474619

# Dedication

*Thank you to my best friend Mark Curriden, a great journalist who continues to inspire.*

*And my family, for helping me pursue my dreams.*

*-Dan*

*To all my friends and colleagues working in the industry, and those who aspire to work in the industry who have no time to read.*

*-Lau*

Copy edits by Patricia Anne Bonaccolta

Final editing by George Lapides, Jeremy Bento and Lau Lapides

# Chapter 1 – Money Management In Media

Talent is not always good at managing or saving money. Actually, many people have a difficult time dealing with money.

But certainly in our industry, we are notorious for being bad at budgeting, not knowing how to deal with making money and that is really the baseline of the business. You have to understand the business aspect. Remember, its show <u>business</u>.

Understand how to do your taxes or hire someone to keep you honest. Balance a budget. Know how to balance your checkbook. These are very basic issues that often times we overlook or think aren't that important. Many industry professionals often say, "We are not going to make enough or we're going to make so much money so we're not going to worry about it." Neither is true.

Understanding your financial matters is as important as the craft itself.

**Lau's Take**

And what is the best way to do that? Should you get help?

The answer is yes. There are plenty of free resources on-line in addition to workshops and seminars provided by industry organizations including unions. There are also untapped resources such as your personal network of parents, close friends, and associates.

For fear of sounding like a financial advisor which I am not, you have to take a moment and really think about how you view money. What does money mean to you in relation to your career? Be prepared even before you land your first job.

**Dan's Take**

If the residual checks or "mailbox money" start pouring in or if you're signing lucrative contracts it is also important for you to know how to budget. The gravy train may be speeding along the rails, but you may reach the station well before you know it.

Don't try to go it alone if you're really not good at it or don't have the time. Seek out professionals who can advise you on income taxes and other important financial decisions.

You might think of it as a big expenditure up front, but it could save you a significant amount of money in the long term.

We are so passionate about what it is that we want to do that we often don't take the time to develop the skills in business. This has left many performers and other media professionals vulnerable.

It is a great and necessary investment.

Budgeting is probably one of the most important things you can do. In your career it is necessary, because there are times where you could make a substantial amount of money and there are times where you will make nothing. Train yourself to be able to live well without overspending and live within your means. These are all things that are going to make you a happier person in the industry when it comes to your finances.

---

Now that we've informed you about the importance of being in control of your finances, our last piece of advice is to negotiate, negotiate, negotiate. It doesn't hurt to push back. Sometimes you will be forced to take less money in order to build your resume. But don't be afraid to push for a little bit more.

It's really about managing your money, managing your career and managing your life.

# Chapter 2 – The Pros And Cons Of Joining A Union

If you don't have a lot of experience with unions and aren't certain about their roles, this is what you should know. Unions like to say that they're around so you won't be standing alone. They watch your back, so they're going to make sure that your contract is adhered to and that you're compensated fairly for your work. The union gives you a floor, a scale, and that is how you know how much you are making and that your pay is protected.

They offer not only protection, but networking opportunities, workshops, auditions, and industry news.

Your membership in a union will open the doors to potential bigger opportunities once you have earned enough to qualify.

On the flip side, some would argue against joining unions. Why? 80%-85% of industry jobs are not unionized. That means the union work is often going to more seasoned professionals. They may not be more talented, but they have more relationships and contacts in place. It's a huge advantage for them and more difficult to overcome.

In addition, you can remain a free agent and can work for anyone at anytime, anywhere. You can negotiate your own contract. And you don't have to pay annual dues however you will find that there are times that you won't have a choice.

**Dan's Take**

When I finally got a job as an NBC News Network correspondent, I was already a union member. That's because in my prior job at a local station in Boston, it was a requirement. Years later, when I joined CNN as a political correspondent and bureau chief, that company wasn't and still to this day, isn't a union shop. My membership was put on hold in good standing. So I think sometimes this question is answered for you when you take a job, but you have to weigh it and ask "What are the benefits long-term for me and do they outweigh any of the cons?"

I have another perspective from the entertainment side. I guest starred on an episode of the hit Fox series, *Bones*. It was an eye-opening experience for someone who had spent decades in the broadcast news business.

As a SAG-AFTRA member I didn't have to worry about my contract and future residuals. All of my earnings are tracked and funneled through my regional union office. It streamlines the process and assures me that my paychecks are issued and received.

The other important thing to consider is to have a conversation with veterans in the industry; ask how has the union worked for them? Then talk to those who are not union members and get an opposing viewpoint. Then make your decision.

**Lau's Take**

I always tell people to visit their local union office. Talk to the union reps (keep in mind it's their job to promote the union). So, do your homework, read through their website. At the same time, talk to non- union industry people and see what their lives are really like. Are they able to make a living? If not, what else are they doing to make ends meet? Are they working at all as a talent?

---

When you're faced with the decision of whether to join the union or not, weigh the pros and cons. Imagine a situation where you might need that kind of support. Ask yourself if you could get that muscle from elsewhere. This information will help make you better prepared to make the right choice.

# Chapter 3 – Work Breeds Work

A lot of people in the industry who are not currently working on a project often fall into the trap of answering, "Nothing," when asked what they are currently working on. That kind of thinking isn't the most effective way to present your brand as active to potential employers.

Because of the internet there are so many opportunities now to publish material, to create your own videos for YouTube, to do your own podcast. These are a few ways to remain actively involved in the industry even if you're not getting paid. Remember you are always working for yourself and your brand.

When you go into an interview, you are often asked, "What are you doing now?" Here are some answers:

I have a podcast. I just published an article. I just released my latest YouTube video, which has already gained thousands of views. I just uploaded my latest web series. I'm taking classes and private coaching sessions. This all shows that you are not just sitting around waiting for the next big thing to hit you over the head. You are creating opportunities for yourself while continuing to gain experience. This approach will help you polish your resume and keep you in the active file.

**Dan's Take**

I like to make an analogy to real estate, where a home that has languished on the market for months with no activity becomes stale in the minds of homebuyers. When a prospective buyer looks at that house the first thing they'll ask an agent is, "What is wrong with the house?" There may be absolutely nothing wrong with it, but the lack of activity gives a much different impression. I think in some ways, when employers are looking to hire someone, they may feel the same way. You want to make sure that you are always active.

**Lau's Take**

I recently had a client in the studio who was very concerned that her acting resume was too thin. So she was not confident enough to pitch herself in follow-up emails or reach out to new contacts. I told her that you're always, always, always working.

Whether you are writing your book, attending training classes, one on one coaching sessions or you are updating your demo reels, you are always working. That way you're communicating that you are not only busy but in demand.

It's a type of energy. You feel it; you sense it. You are not transmitting the vibe that you're lazy or waiting for something to happen. You find joy and inspiration in movement and your energy is keeping the machine well oiled, so to speak. It also makes you happier and tells the world that you are fully engaged in what you are doing because you want to be, not because you are waiting for someone to come in and make you famous.

If you are occupying your time doing things that will advance your career then from a mental standpoint, it is also a lot healthier.

Set some goals that you can truly achieve and that are not based or contingent on other people. It is really you internally setting up those goals and achieving them.

There are times that you will be cast in small and seemingly insignificant roles, but you get to meet casting directors, agents, crew or other people in the industry. All those contacts may open important doors in the future.

---

Ultimately, when you develop a strong work ethic, it automatically separates you from the crowd. Employers will feel that sense of focus and ambition. That's the kind of attention that could make a big difference in your career.

# Chapter 4: Ready, Set, Go!

Be careful what you wish for you may get it. You want to get that role, that job; you want to get your foot in the door. Suddenly you get a call. Are you prepared for it? You must be ready to respond quickly with your resume, headshot and cover letter.

**Lau's Take**

We were assisting a casting director for a high level regional voice over gig. It paid well and offered an excellent opportunity for a live audition experience with a popular studio. This job was time sensitive. We carefully selected a handful of top talent, many of whom we know personally and a few of them are our clients. Amazingly, only a fraction of the people we reached out to actually responded. And only a fraction of those people responded within the time limit. These folks were either too busy or not ready to jump at this great opportunity. Often times these are the same people who will later complain that they aren't getting enough work.

**Dan's Take**

Much like a firefighter who is ready at a moment's notice when the call or email comes in respond as quickly as possible. The truck must always be polished; the tanks must always be filled with fuel and water to head out the door.

There should be no scrambling or excuses such as "I need to update my reel," "My profile page isn't up to date," "I need a new headshot or I'm too busy."

We hear this all too often. Success means having professional training behind you, continually doing your homework and being ready when opportunities come to you. If you can't make it when an opportunity arises, at the very least respond to the request immediately.

---

Industry professionals appreciate and often reward those who are organized and respond with a quick turnaround. There are hundreds of people waiting to get a call and your delay could cost you an audition or a job.

# Chapter 5 – Value Personal Relationships

Unlike 9 to 5 jobs, this industry is 24/7. Sometimes you work at odd hours and far away locations for extended periods of time. It is at times difficult to deal with the fluctuating nature of this industry. You are often called away on the spur of the moment because there's an opportunity to work.

This balancing act can take a toll on relationships and requires the support and understanding of family and friends.

**Dan's Take**

The way that I have dealt with this is to be up front and recognize it as a challenge that comes with an amazing adventure; something that I can share with the people closest to me.

This often chaotic lifestyle meant for me, a relationship with someone who was in the business and understood what came with the job. When I got called to breaking news stories, she understood. We started driving separate cars to social functions, anticipating a call to be available as quickly as possible. What made our relationship work is constant communication and a contingency plan.

**Lau's Take**

I love that; you took the words right out of my mouth. Communication is your best friend. It's what you need to be doing. Make sure your network of people fully understand the demands of this lifestyle. If you are raising children in families where there's so much unplanned last minute travel and uncertain schedules, it requires frequent conversations.

I've had many clients and colleagues who have relationships with people who unfortunately drag them down with responsibilities and their attitudes. They're unhappy with the lack of consistency and are unwilling to compromise.

Don't ignore this issue. It won't go away.

The understanding must extend to the financial ups and downs that come with this career. One month you may be making good money. Another couple of months you may not bring home a dime.

This is a much different environment from the steady paycheck that lands in your account every two weeks.

---

The bottom line is the more preparation that you can make ahead of time, long before you are faced with any of these issues, the better it will be for your relationship. In addition, if you already have your career path cemented, be honest and transparent before jumping into relationships. Paint a clear picture of the dedication and time commitment that this industry requires. Keep surprises to a minimum and your relationships will fare a lot better.

# Chapter 6 – Stay Local Or Go National?

There is no right or wrong answer to this question, but there are some important issues to consider.

Staying in a smaller media market where the spotlight isn't as bright will allow you to develop your skills, and make and survive mistakes.

It may also be more economically feasible to build your career in a locally focused market. Everything from housing to industry standard materials will be more affordable. Take advantage of this opportunity; squeeze the juice out of it before making the leap to a bigger stage.

On a personal level are you ready to tackle the rigors of a more competitive playing field?

**Lau's Take**

When a client sits down with us and says, "I want to move to Hollywood," (or any other hot market) we find, more often than not is that they have no level of understanding of what the industry standard is and how difficult it is to compete in such a crowded field. It doesn't mean they shouldn't make the move, but are they prepared? Ask yourself, are you a quick learner? Do you have the skills that will allow you to essentially scale up very quickly to that market level.

**Dan's Take**

When I was working in Chattanooga, my first job out of graduate school, I was offered a new job in a larger market within a few months. I carefully weighed the pros and cons. Yes, it was going to be huge leap for my career, but I wasn't ready. I knew I still needed to strengthen my skills and make mistakes before branching out. That meant staying put for another year.

---

When you feel that you are ready and have done the research, a good piece of advice is test the market. Spend a little time there. Gauge the level of competition and get a clear picture of the economics. Finally, make sure this is a place that you would be happy to spend the next few years building your career.

# Chapter 7 – The Art Of Cold Calling

The worst that can happen when you make a cold call to a talent agent or manager is to be told, "No thank you," or, "Not at this time." If you don't ask, the answer will always be "No." Yet so many people are stopped dead in their tracks by the fear of rejection. The myth is a lot more frightening than reality. The reality is taking that step could open doors for you.

Fear nothing when it comes to reaching out to potential new relationships. Often agents and casting directors will say, "Why don't we follow up in a month or two," or "We might need you in the future and don't want to say no right now."

**Lau's Take**

I can't even recall how many times in the past 10 or 15 years that someone has told me "No." But it hasn't stopped me. I keep trying and for every "no" I encounter there have been plenty of positive responses often leading to work.

I also have the habit of circling back with a new pitch and have found some takers!

Years ago, I wanted to attend a local college, but wasn't accepted. I was disappointed and frankly devastated. Here's the beauty of it all: I was eventually contacted and asked to teach a course at the very same place that had turned me away! What do you suppose that course was? "How to Make It in the Business for the Performer." I was able to sprinkle in examples of how I personally overcame career disappointments. I moved through that perceived obstacle as if it didn't exist and had the last word.

**Dan's Take**

One of the little tricks that I use when cold calling is to think up the best-case scenario. I figure this person will become a great connection or give me an incredible opportunity. It is all a mental game but I use it as motivation.

For instance, I reached out to a complete stranger on LinkedIn. Their profile was appealing and appeared to have a lot in common with some of my profession goals.

That "cold call" that I visualized as a home run, lead to an in-depth conversation and just like that I made a solid connection. Within a few days I had established a great business opportunity.

---

Another trick to ease the discomfort of cold calling is to do a little research into the person you are calling and identify things you have in common. Do you come from the same town or attended the same college. Do you both share a passion for racing or skiing? Everyone has something in common if you dig a little bit. Opening your call with that common thread could be the door into a great opportunity.

Visualize success, reach out and success will happen.

# Chapter 8 – Be Knowledgeable About Your Contract

It is always astounding, and we don't use that word lightly, how many industry professionals don't even know what's in their contract. They "skim" it, don't read it, or have blind trust that it was written in their best interest.

Before we go a step further here's an obvious but important piece of advice: CAREFULLY READ YOUR CONTRACT IN ITS ENTIRETY! If you don't understand it, take it to a lawyer, a manager, a coach, or a friend with knowledge in this area. Don't count on a conversation, what the person across the table has told you that you would be paid or what you would be required to do as part of the deal. Just know that in a court of law, your transaction is going to be about what is written in that contract and not what was said.

There are many resources that don't require money and can save you time and headaches. Reach out to a law school in your area. Often time's students can assist with basic legal needs. There are also low cost online options that can assist you with translating some of the complex language in your contract.

**Dan's Take**

People have bad habits when it comes to contracts in everyday life. At rental car agencies, I see everyone signing without reading the fine print. I always take the time to not only read what I am signing, but ask questions if I don't understand something. I want to make sure that when I wrap the car around the tree it is paid for by the right party. So what if the people on the other side of the counter get annoyed if I take the time to read it? It is my wallet on the line.

**Lau Take**

While it is important to have a complete understanding of your contract there is a limit to how far you should go and how much time should be spent going back and forth over every minor detail.

I had a client who didn't take the time to consult a network of appropriate people to help vet her contract and instead went overboard in haggling with a new agent. It was like a tennis match. Revisions and requests went back and forth until the agent in frustration dropped them and canceled their contract. The deal was dead before it even got started.

---

Among the most important things to pay attention to in your contract is exclusivity. Are you locked into working only with that agent, manager or studio or are you able to freelance? If you are exclusive then the question should be for how long? And is the contract automatically self-renewing?

Know the difference. A lot of good opportunities have been lost because someone didn't pay attention to their contract.

# Chapter 9 – It's Never Too Early To Start

Graduation day is often filled with big speeches about taking on life's challenges and finally putting knowledge to the test in your respective fields. However, if you are waiting for your diploma to get started in your career you might just be a tad late. As soon as you figure out what you enjoy or are passionate about that is when you should start working.

One way to do that is through an internship. Finding the right fit requires a bit of research. Seek out companies that will offer hands-on opportunities – either for school credit or stipend – rather than just well known organizations that often restrict how much work you can actually do and experience. Filing documents or making copies of meeting notes may not be the best opportunity to build your career.

**Lau's Take**

I can't emphasize this point enough. Doing as much work as possible early on will increase your skills and your value to a potential employer. It also gives you the opportunity to determine whether this is the path you truly want to pursue and that it is the kind of environment that you want to work in.

Use this time to also sell yourself. How? When it comes to skills in technology, a younger person may have an advantage like understanding and utilizing social media for marketing purposes or using the latest tools to communicate.

**Dan's Take**

I completely agree with Lau on the value of a good internship. In addition, there are other options to gain experience and make contacts.

There are plenty of workshops you can attend in person or online. Read as much as possible about the industry and the strategies some of the most successful people are using. Take any and all opportunities to network. That may not seem like a huge deal, but people I met along the way later offered me great opportunities helped my career immensely. It helps you move ahead of others in line when you already have some momentum based on these steps.

Don't wait for your first official job to kick off your career. Blogging is a way of honing your writing skills and potentially gaining a broad audience. There are plenty of examples of people who jumped straight from a blog to a major publication. Online video sites are another way to showcase your acting, producing, writing, photography and other media talents. Again, it costs very little if anything and you get a chance to make mistakes and learn from them, as well as an opportunity to gain an audience and catch the eye of the right person.

---

The bottom line is put your career in motion while still in basic training. There is much to gain and little to risk. What you choose to do in taking action in this moment may affect and indicate the path you will land on for your future career. Everything you do, every move you make may lead to something else.

# Chapter 10 – Making A Memorable Impression

Making a memorable first impression doesn't begin when you open your mouth during an audition or interview. It starts when you walk into the room. You make an instant impact during your first three to five seconds.

It's not to say that the first impression will make or break you, but the people that you are in front of are often very seasoned. They are fluent in your body language. They know when someone is professional and put together, meaning, someone who is thoughtful about the way they present themselves. It speaks volumes about your ability to do the job and they can figure that out very quickly. It may not always be accurate or fair, but they know what they want and time is of the essence.

### Dan's Take

You want to be as authentic as possible but at the same time look for ways to shift and blend, to meet your audience's needs. That may require tweaking your wardrobe, hairstyle or makeup. The visual sometimes may be more powerful than anything that comes out of your mouth and could determine whether you get the role or not. I've heard some people say, "this is who I am. I like wearing my hair this way and this is my style." That is all good, unless you end up attracting attention – for the wrong reason- to yourself instead of the job itself. Think of yourself as a product and the person you are going before as a customer. Know what they like and are looking for and package yourself accordingly.

### Lau's Take

It's also important to listen to the feedback that you get either at the audition or from outside voices. If you don't get a role or job don't be afraid to ask, "What could I have done better?" or "What is it about my brand that needs a facelift?" Maybe it is something that you weren't aware of. People in your inner circle sometimes miss the obvious too. Asking those questions could help you refine your non-verbal pitch and identify problems that may be clouding your brand such as changing your makeup, the colors you wear, improving your posture or fixing your teeth.

---

It's great to have people around who recognize your greatness and validate your choices, but a healthy dose of professional review is important. This is where having a qualified manager, agent or coach can make the difference. Don't be afraid to ask their opinion. More importantly listen to their feedback and make the adjustments.

Remember that the clock is ticking when you walk in the room. Don't confuse those sitting on the other side of the table and give them a reasons to be distracted.

# Chapter 11 – Be Bold And Take Chances

If you are going to succeed in this business you must be willing to take risks - calculated risks. Don't be afraid to step out of your comfort zone and push yourself. No risk = no reward. The first step to taking risks is being open and somewhat vulnerable and ready for the unknown. This is an integral part of being creative and career driven.

**Lau's Take**

You must be brave and a little bit fearless in this industry. Develop courage like the Lion in the Wizard of Oz. It's very important for you to develop that inner strength. You shouldn't feel like everything is life or death, or everything is a personal attack when it doesn't work out. You should be ready for anything. There have been so many times when I hesitated or thought about not pushing forward because I didn't want to fail. In just about every case taking that bold step led to bigger rewards. Now to be honest that's not always guaranteed, but if you don't push you won't discover what you're capable of doing.

**Dan's Take**

I've found that some people are afraid to try something bold because not only is there the risk of failure but also ridicule. Will you be painted as a failure? Will the roles or opportunities you attempted outweigh the one's you got? That can paralyze some people. In my case, there were many fears. At my first job I had to ask myself if I was ready to become an education reporter? Should I push to sit in the anchor chair? Then a few years later, should I jump to a broadcast network with millions of eyes watching every story? In every step there was apprehension. But that never held me back from pushing those walls out of the way.

---

Make sure it's not reckless boldness. You must be prepared and qualified for that new role.

Think of it this way, dealing with fear is part of the process. This isn't a business that operates in the shadows.

Yes, there are many people who are behind the scenes. However, the public and critics watch every production and/or product closely. Manage those dark thoughts but don't let them become an obstacle to achieving your goals. Use that energy as motivation.

# Chapter 12 – One Decision Can Change Your Life

Never underestimate the power of one decision and the potential that it can bring you. This is easier to understand when you look in life's rearview mirror. Making the effort to attend a trade show or an industry mixer could make an enormous difference in launching your career. That's why you must be thoughtful with every opportunity and every introduction that comes your way.

## Lau's Take

I always talk to our clients about sitting next to that person in the airplane or on the bus. You may or may not want a conversation, but that person next to you could turn into a client or great connection. He or she could be so well connected and know a lot of people with whom you're going to want to work. Not engaging could be a missed opportunity. Big breaks don't just come from job interviews and casting calls they come from small moments that happen in a blink of the eye.

## Dan's Take

I met a good contact on a flight to the West Coast. While he didn't change the course of my career, years later he became a valuable business contact. That was huge for me because I rely on air travel as my respite space. Even though technology makes it easier for us to stay connected even in the air, I like to unplug and be still. Another time, a friend suggested a meeting with a company that had no job openings. It made no sense at the time, but that meeting put me on the course that eventually led to an agent who managed my career for the next two decades.

Would things have turned out as well had I not gone to that early meeting? I don't know, perhaps not. But you have to be alert to these different kinds of opportunities because just that one decision, taking one job over another, determined what I became.

---

This is a tough one because you can't be everywhere all the time and often you're just too tired to commit to every opportunity. However, keep in mind that it's all about the little everyday decisions that we make about our careers.

Those big things do matter too, but pay attention to seemingly mundane things. Should I introduce myself to this person, attend that cocktail party, send a thank you note or make a cold call? You must be open and aware. It's not just up to fate and luck.

# Chapter 13 – The Power Of Saying "No"

You don't have to say yes to everything. You can't do it all. Even great opportunities may not be right for you, so don't be afraid to say no. There are times when financial pressures dictate that you do more than you should or care to, because there's little choice. Rent needs to be paid, food must be put on the table, and there are some of those pressing business expenses that must be covered.

However, a healthy career flourishes when you know how to take a step back.

## Lau's Take

I think "no" has the power of protecting you. "No" is setting healthy boundaries. "No" is not doing things you're truly and deeply uncomfortable with in your career.

It's tempting to always say yes, but you could end up imbalanced, exhausted and too depleted to get to the next level.

This is a bad habit I see repeated over and over again. There is a common fear that downtime is wasted time and always being available is the way to go. But, there are times when saying "no" may open the door for more opportunities simply because you are available.

## Dan's Take

I remember working at a television station that required me to stay plugged in 24/7. As a young reporter with few outside responsibilities, I always went above and beyond. It seemed the best way to advance my career. But one morning, exhausted after a breaking news wake-up call put me in front of the camera for hours, I made some critical mistakes that could have been avoided. It was the result of always saying "yes" to everything that was asked of me. What I learned was that it can directly affect the quality of your work. You're doing so much that you're not doing anything well. You have to make sure that there is a healthy balance. And sometimes a big part of that balance is saying "no."

**Lau's Take**

It's not always easy. There are those of us who are part of the Workaholic's Anonymous Club and I am the president.

Dan: Yeah and I am the vice president.

Lau: Always pleasing and never saying "no" is a bad habit and it can turn into an addiction and go from an asset to a deficit very, very quickly.

---

We mentioned in an earlier chapter that part of the secret to success is staying active, always doing something so that it appears to the person who wants to hire you or is thinking about hiring you that you are in demand. But there's a real danger of burnout. If you find yourself in this situation, audit your calendar. Take a real hard look at whether what you are doing is building your career, bringing in money or hurting you in the long run. We all love what we do. We want to do it all the time. But beware of depleting yourself and just say no.

# Chapter 14 – The Power Of Saying "Yes"

In the previous chapter, we made the case for the advantages of saying "no." However, saying "yes" to opportunities and being known as the person who doesn't complain is often a great asset to your career. You may not always be the most skilled person for the job. There may be others with longer, healthier, more robust resumes, but you may move to the front of the line because those who hire you know what they are going to get. The impression you will give to them is, "If we hire this person, they'll be easy to work with, agreeable and do a great job."

**Dan's Take**

Be the one to raise your hand. Be the one to go at a moment's notice. Early on I developed the reputation as someone who was reliable and available to move quickly without hesitation. Saying "yes" opened many doors for me.  In just about every job I've held there is always that one person well known for saying "NO!" They always have something to do and everywhere to go. Granted, some of their excuses could have been legitimate, but they developed a reputation that was difficult to shake. What often happens is that when it comes time to downsize staff or send team on a great assignment Mr. or Ms. "No" will fall behind.

**Lau's Take**

It's really is all about having a great attitude, being fully accountable and just trying. You're not always going to be completely successful. It doesn't mean you're going to be comfortable and it doesn't always mean they're going to ask you to do it again. It means that you are willing to try and do and learn and progress. There's something very powerful about that mindset. Don't mistake this with being a "yes man." This is not about refusing to push back on something that you disagree with. This is about raising your hand to do your job and a bit extra even if you don't always feel like it.

---

Be honest with yourself. Try very hard to lose the excuses. If you don't think this chapter pertains to you then do this exercise: Think of all the excuses you have ever given your boss.

Write them down. "I'm tired," "I've never done that before," "It's not my job to do that." You get the point. How long is your list? This visual exercise may be the wakeup call you need to start saying YES a lot more than NO.

Work to free yourself of those excuses so that you can allow growth and true potential to happen.

# Chapter 15 – Dealing With Rejection

Everyone has been rejected at one time or another, unless you're very lucky and you hit home runs every time. Rejection isn't pretty and never feels good, but remember it's not always a loss. Rejection can be more positive than it appears. It often opens the door to something better. You don't have to do that much research into most successful companies or industry professionals to see how they turned failure into triumph. Some companies were on their last dime. Nothing seemed to work until they finally learned from their mistakes and were able to grow. Performers and most talent in the industry tell stories of how they learned to handle rejection that came more often, than not.

**Lau's Take**

I know it's not easy, but try not to take rejection personally. Of course, there are times when someone doesn't like you or care for your audition, but often it's less about that than it is about timing and what they are looking for. In three months, you could be the perfect fit. After every rejection sit down and make a list of all the things that you did right. It's like your personal pep rally. Keep a file of stories of famous people who have been rejected. Read an article or two. It's good to fill your mind with positive messages instead of dwelling on rejection.

**Dan's Take**

I love to tell the story of Katie Couric and how a news director harshly rejected her and told her she'd never make it in the news business. We know how that turned out.

Then there's the example of my wife. She also wanted to be a news anchor and was told by a news manager at a small station that she wasn't the right material. Instead of giving up completely she discovered her stronger skills were behind the camera, not in front of it. She went on to become a producer at the network level, ironically working on stories for Katie Couric.

In both cases rejection turned out to be a good thing. For Couric, it became motivation. For my wife, it uncovered her real strengths as a producer.

How should you react when faced with rejection?

The professional is the one who when slammed with rejection gets up, dusts themselves off and then uses that experience to make it to the next round. The amateur stays on the ropes, surrenders and may literally quit trying in the industry.

Be the professional. Use that competitive edge to prove your critics wrong, improve your skills or shift direction.

# Chapter 16 – How To Work Both Well In A Team & Independently

A team can motivate, inspire and surround you with energy to thrive. Working independently offers an unparalleled level of flexibility and control. The challenge is how to make the best of both worlds. One isn't better than the other. It all depends on your line of work and often times your personality.

**Lau's Take**

When you're self-employed you have to brace yourself for a level of loneliness and isolation. There are several ways to deal with that. First, realize that you are a business. That will require you to put in place a structure that works best and is most productive for you. Second, you are your best representative so your approach to meeting people, marketing, auditioning, etc. should be aggressive and strategic. Third, create a circle of contacts and people who are like-minded and who will be a rich resource when called upon.

**Dan's Take**

Here's something that's worked for me. I think when you are working by yourself, there has to be a process. One day a week I do a phone check-in with someone who is in the same industry and we chat about the previous week. "How are things going?" "How did you do moneywise?" "Did you make any new contacts?" "What were some stumbling blocks?" "Let me tell you about the challenges that I faced." It is a helpful way to stay connected and aware while inspiring and motivating each other.

As part of a team it's critical to quickly adjust even if the time period is only one day or a few weeks, practice walking into a room with a group of strangers. Strike a balance between confidence and attitude. It's very important to listen to what they have to say and understand how to respond appropriately and effectively when called upon.

Approach the team members as colleagues, not necessarily new friends.

Determine the group's strengths and weaknesses then figure out how you can contribute to the team and how that team can contribute to your success.

There will be times in this industry filled with big egos, where personalities clash. You have to be able to go in and say, "I am okay with that. I can work with difficult people. I can work with easy people. I can do that." That is a skill.

---

As in many of the key points we raise in this book, it's always good to "interview" industry veterans to seek out additional advice. Learn tips that have helped them manage either working solo or as part of a team. That kind of real time information from someone in a similar job is priceless.

Whether you are working independently or within a group, following these steps will help you navigate the terrain more smoothly and reach your destination successfully.

# Chapter 17 – Learn Something New Every Day

What did you learn today? Did you read or hear something for the first time? You might have a lofty college degree and register off the charts on IQ tests, but a mindset of constant learning can be a healthy thing for your career. Wake up every day with a thirst for growth and knowledge. Try something different that reboots your life. Read and consume information. Stay connected. Plug yourself into the media. Pay attention to your industry and keep yourself relevant.

**Lau's Take**

Stay fresh. You should be on top of the areas in which you want to be working. If you want to be in an episodic, then watch the episodics. If you want to be in a sitcom, binge watch sitcoms that are out there right now. Study the roles that appeal to you. Pay attention to acting styles, directing, language and scripts, and really have an awareness of what is current today.

My studio had a workshop with a top voiceover animation star. He asked the group, "What is your favorite cartoon?" The crowd was silent. When prodded, someone said, "Well I don't really watch TV." Our guest replied, "Then you shouldn't be going into this business, because you don't appear interested enough to do your homework. How can you develop your own career?"

**Dan's Take**

At the end of the day, around the dinner table with my family, we often ask each other if we learned anything new at work or at school. This conversation reinforces the importance of opening and expanding our minds constantly with new things. Some of these experiences may transform your life and a lot of these things may help your career, but you have to be open to it. You have to be in that mindset of, "Today is not going to be like any other day. Today is going to be a fresh, new day with new opportunities, new knowledge and a chance to start again fresh."

---

Stay curious. Stay inquisitive. Stay interesting. You want to be one of the most well informed people in your world. This will open doors.

# Chapter 18 - Turning An Internship Into A Job

Hollywood is littered with wonderful stories of people who started in the mailroom as interns and worked their way up to the top. It's a good example of how you should regard an internship. It gives you the opportunity to get to know the landscape and the players. You get access as an intern to places, people and things that would be difficult otherwise. Use your position wisely and think of it as more than just fetching coffee and making copies. Take copious notes, remember names, meet people and attend parties and events. Figure out where the biggest need is, then focus on learning as much as possible in that area and jump in to assist. That strategy may help you to get noticed and perhaps eventually lead to a job.

**Dan's Take**

I once had an intern who was proficient in the early days of social media; something us adults weren't well versed in at the time. She suggested using the MySpace platform to find a key interview. I pushed aside my doubts and told her to do her thing. It was like magic. We immediately found three options. That was one of the standout moments that led me to go to bat for her. She eventually was hired at the company and continues to thrive at a major network. That is the magic of turning an internship into a full-time job. Another intern wanted to learn about editing and worked for months for free only to develop the expertise that put veteran editors to shame. That editor was eventually hired and is thriving in the industry to this day.

**Lau's Take**

As an intern, you should make yourself invaluable, have a great attitude and make it clear that you're not only hungry to learn, but also have a lot to contribute. You should not be afraid to speak up, nor assume that the bosses know exactly what they want from you. Express your interests. Just because you're working as intern that doesn't mean you don't have a voice. Don't just fit in; stand out.

This is all especially important as more and more big companies are looking to a younger workforce to help them navigate the latest technology and understand youthful trends. High school students, college students or recent graduates produced some of the most shared content on social media. The days of relying solely on institutional employees are gone. Take advantage of this to maximize your internship and turn it into a job if not a great career.

# Chapter 19 – Knowing When To Hold 'Em And Fold 'Em

There are two schools of thought about knowing when to hold 'em and when to fold 'em. The first path involves being tenacious, never giving up and being resilient. That may require a thick skin so that you can move forward towards your goals. Understand it's going to be difficult and take time to achieve, but you can make it fun. You're going to learn and you're going to do what you want to do, so don't give up too quickly because it takes time to really develop your true potential. On the other hand, you don't want to waste years of precious time if you're not getting any traction. It may be proof that it's time to rethink your goals and perhaps consider moving in a different direction.

**Dan's Take**

It happens often at that darkest moment when you're right around the corner from success. Often people will just throw their hands up and make drastic changes out of emotion and exasperation. They end up working at something that they're not happy with and if they'd only kept on going they would have reached that point where progress started to pay off.

I can't tell you how many times I've doubted my directional skills while searching for an address and then turned off the road too early, right before I got to the correct intersection.

It can be so frustrating. All that driving got me to one block away… am I throwing time and effort away? All I had to do was crawl one more block and I would have gotten to my destination. There are times when you must persevere and not surrender too early just because it is too tough.

**Lau's Take**

I often get this question from clients: Should I quit at this point? My philosophy is that it's not my job, as a coach to give a yes or no answer. What I can suggest is that you ask yourself the following questions:

What have I really accomplished? Make a list to help you think back over the past weeks, months or years.

How much time and money have I invested? This will help you understand the cost benefit of your financial decisions. How strong is my network? This will help you determine if you have just been showing up for interviews and auditions without making the effort to cement some relationships. Be honest with yourself. If you find that your answers are lacking, then you haven't been proactive enough to get to that level of success.

---

Asking some tough questions will help you decide to either double down or conclude that you don't have the time, energy or capital to keep plugging away. Remember; don't make the decision too hastily. Be sure you are satisfied with your efforts and are reaching towards realistic goals. A false sense of what is possible could be distorting your definition of progress.

# Chapter 20 – Optimism

We're talking about creating an optimistic mindset and attitude and cultivating it daily. So many people have failed in their careers because they always focus on what isn't possible instead on what is. Learn to see the glass as half full and not half empty. This old adage may seem trite, but it's very true.

When you have an optimistic attitude, you build momentum that can lead to success. It is something that people will see. Bosses will notice. Casting directors and all those folks who will be potentially be signing your paycheck will feel it. It not only helps you to be healthier in general, but will make you more marketable.

### Lau's Take

People will gravitate towards you. In our industry, we use elusive terms like magnetic, charismatic and attractive. What does it really mean? Is it just about the way you look? The way you sound? Your attitude, mindset, energy and vibe all have a direct effect on the other people whom you are dealing with. It is why they like to work with you and tend to call you. They think of you as a go-to person who will solve their problems and fill their needs.

### Dan's Take

I recently met a fitness guru who defined the ideal of positive attitude. There was a certain vibe about him. Even before our conversation began at a local coffee house I was ready to buy into whatever he had to say. That was the key to his success. He has a thriving business helping people get physically fit from the inside out. You feel compelled to plug into his energy and vision, much like recharging your phone.

Harvard Business School has traditionally asked incoming students about their positive mental attitude, emphasizing how necessary it is, not only to make it through the program, but as a powerful tool in the success of their careers.

In addition to polishing your resume, maintain your optimism. Why? In corporate environments as well as in the media industry, this is increasingly becoming an important factor along with education and experience. This is the internal engine that pushes some people further along than others who are too quick to surrender even before they begin.  An optimistic attitude and mindset is also contagious. Flaunt it and pass it on.

# Chapter 21 – Wear Many Hats And Diversify

It's always important to choose your area of expertise, but also to become a jack-of-all-trades. The more you know, the more valuable you become. If you've ever worked in a startup or read about entrepreneurs the reality is that everyone has to do many tasks in order for the company to succeed. Long before a full team is in place or a product gets to market the CEO may have to be the accountant and the head of sales and marketing. Learn to think like an entrepreneur, because that is exactly what you are.

**Dan's Take**

We know that focus is important. It's helpful in honing your skills and steering you to the right career moves. However, if you're in front of the camera in a sound booth, or working behind the scenes, being flexible and handling many different roles diversifies your portfolio and makes you more attractive. It could expand your job and income options. That's especially true since technology makes it easier for one person to do the job that used to require a small crew to accomplish.

**Lau's Take**

You're going to have to frequently balance many tasks. That's just the nature of what we do. It's no longer about just one thing. What you must figure out is how to manage your time without getting overwhelmed. You also must leave your ego at the door and be willing to take on a job that you never expected to do. There are some actors who now carry cameras and produce small budget projects for social media. There are TV journalists who focus solely on reporting and now travel the world shooting, producing and editing their own work. Voice-over artists have learned to become their own engineers in their home studios.

---

If you're having trouble diversifying your skills to make yourself more marketable there are plenty of low-cost adult learning centers, libraries, community colleges and online programs that offer courses in a variety of areas.

Do a little research and find out what's trending in your area. This will help you decide where to spend your time and effort to better increase your chances of finding consistent work.

# Chapter 22 – How To Multitask With Success

Are you terrified of your daily schedule? You wake up facing a mile-long list of things that have to get done and you can't seem to see the end of the tunnel? That's the classic multi-tasking dilemma.

But, like a proficient circus performer there are ways to juggle many balls in the air without having them crash to the ground.

Begin by setting priorities. Don't take on more than you can handle and do well. Then begin to organize. Don't be afraid to ask for help. That's not a sign of weakness. It's a sign of success.

### Lau's Take

When it comes to multitasking most people are not able to really deal with the challenges that come with this skill. It's hard to be efficient in this fast-paced demanding industry. One way to get around that is to be prepared. Structure yourself and know what you need. For instance, a software scheduling program, accounting services and in-home studios are all tools that will help you get the job(s) done. Give yourself a separate personal office space to work in. Again, it will help with organization.

### Dan's Take

Getting a separate office space made a world of difference in my entrepreneurial endeavors. And inside that office, the most sacred things to me are my white boards. I have several of them. Lots of color markers help me multitask between projects. The boards are constantly there at eye level so I can keep track of what has been done, what I'm working on presently and what projects need to be tackled next.

---

This doesn't mean that from time to time one ball may not hit the floor, but putting together an effective infrastructure allows you to move forward without too much disruption. Finally, sticky notes are a cheap and easy way to help you multi task. Stick them on things that need to be done. Every time you see that bright square of paper you will be reminded to do that task. It keeps things from falling through the cracks.

# Chapter 23 – Set Achievable Goals

In an earlier chapter we warned about having a false sense of what is possible because it could be distorting your definition of progress or success. To that end, while it's great to shoot for the moon because that is when great things can happen, you must remain realistic.

Be honest with yourself. Use the lofty goals to motivate you and some amazing things will happen on the journey. Making it to the proverbial summit is great, but there are all too many successful people hanging around near the top too.

### Lau's Take

You have to learn to understand what you can achieve. To do that you should sit down with your advisor or coach and write down your short-term (the low hanging fruit) and long term goals (which require more time and attention), then ask "Can I really achieve these? What do I need to make it happen?" When you develop a roadmap based on your answers it will make the path forward much easier. Sometimes the path you want to take isn't the most realistic for your skill set. Making a pivot could propel you forward faster.

### Dan's Take

At some point down the road, re-evaluate your goals. Recognize that they may shift throughout your career. Don't be afraid to make changes even if you have invested time and money in one area that seems to be working but not thriving. Sometimes holding on to those original goals can become more problematic. So, make the adjustments that are needed.

We realize that there have been amazing inventions and advances beginning with overly ambitious goals. Long before technology caught up, someone was thinking about bringing 3-D to the big screen or putting a camera in a phone to give the world equal access to making home videos. Someone had to imagine color when everyone was thinking black and white. So pushing the limits of what is possible is healthy, but be realistic and understand the risks of pushing too hard too far.

Finally, don't be discouraged when someone questions your goals. Again, a lot of people have been told by the experts that they wouldn't make it. Many casting, directors, and talent agents have turned away people who later became A-listers. Publishers have rejected authors who went onto deliver blockbusters. Sometimes you might be just ahead of the times, but ultimately only you know what's possible.

# Chapter 24 – Get Ready To Be Uncomfortable

What kind of lifestyle do you want to live? What do you want to have in your life to make it comfortable? How many material items do you need to make you happy?

These are all questions that will require a bit of soul searching on your part, but are important to ask especially if you're not prepared to be uncomfortable in everyday life and career.

Some people get lucky. Instant celebrity! They land a substantial role right off the bat, make a lot of money and get steady work until retirement. Then there are those who may not be stars, but have built a solid portfolio of work over time and continue to make a good living.

However, the majority of people in this industry begin with big dreams but struggle to keep their heads above water as they go from gig to gig. It's a mix of waiting tables, walking pets and temp office jobs.

As anyone who has achieved any level of success knows that it takes years and years to build your business brand and be viewed as successful.

A willingness to compromises and live a low budget lifestyle can be in some ways a job requirement.

## Lau's Take

In order to help avoid some of the stress that results from over extending yourself and feeling the pressure of needing tons and tons of money to cover your monthly expenses, you should begin by thinking less is more. By simplifying your life and not living beyond your means, you're able to devote more time to your career, set solid goals and get things done.

## Dan's Take

I remember early in my career when I was still paying off college debt and on a strict budget, I frankly didn't want to have a roommate. But I had to be realistic and financially responsible. Since my salary was less than minimal, working in a small local TV news market, I knew I had to share an apartment in order to live a halfway comfortable life.

I'm very neat and like to keep everything in its place. My roommate would walk in the front door, drop all his clothes on the floor and jump in the shower.

That lifestyle was very uncomfortable for me. In addition, I couldn't maintain my car and so I was hitching rides or riding my bike.

Through it all I stayed focused on my goal. I was passionate about what I was doing and was prepared to make sacrifices, until I became able to upgrade my situation and become a little bit more comfortable.

---

Think of being uncomfortable as a temporary condition. Use it to motivate yourself to push harder, to fight and struggle for that big break. Then throw in a dash of patience as you achieve another level in your career.

# Chapter 25 – Surviving A Chaotic Industry

This industry produces a huge amount of top quality, high budget content. When the public sees the finished product, it is smooth and polished.

However behind the scenes more often than not you will be facing controlled chaos.

For those of you just getting started, or even seasoned veterans, it can be shocking how any project ever makes it to the finish line and gets completed.

There are oversized personalities with different creative ideas. It's very common in our industry to experience shouting, screaming, name-calling and factions undermining each other. Things that one couldn't get away with in the "normal" corporate world are overlooked and brushed off as "gifted" or "visionary." We are, after all, working in the arts. High ratings and box office success help to push this highly emotional culture along.

But we live with it because opportunities are highly competitive and ruffling feathers can be bad for your career.

**Lau's Take**

You have to understand that many people in this industry are very emotional and highly visceral. Realize that oftentimes they are wearing their emotions on their sleeve and shooting from the hip. Perhaps they are simply having a bad moment or are overly excited. In the next minute, everything changes.

**Dan's Take**

If you are intimidated by this amount of noise and chaos in the workplace, your tolerance level will help determine how long you can survive and how far you can go. Clearly there are workplace laws that protect you from some of the more extreme personalities out there. But understanding how to navigate this atmosphere is essential. One way that I've learned to cope is to not take things too personally. I grew a turtle-like shell to shield myself from some of the turmoil. I also realize now that it's beneficial from time to time to have an edge and push back.

---

Keep in mind that in the end the product gets made and like in sports, the clash usually stays on the field.

# Chapter 26 – Don't Sell Out Your Morals And Ethics

This is probably one of the most important chapters in our book. People coming into the industry and those who have been working for a while are challenged at times with roles and projects that teeter on the gray line. It may be the wardrobe or lack thereof, inappropriate language and questionable content. Perhaps it's the sketchy reputation of an agent or manager that makes one uncomfortable from the get-go.

**Lau's Take**

Here's an example: It's common for women to be asked to do nudity for a project. It's as common as being asked "Would you like a latte?" For some, this is a moral dilemma that requires careful consideration. Others may be comfortable with nudity in the right context or are willing to push their limits if the money is right. Wherever that line is for you, know that whatever is put out there into the ether is going to stay out there forever. You can never take it back.

**Dan's Take**

I have never been asked to pose nude, in fact, I have been asked to put on more clothes.

[Lau quips] That can't be true.

But seriously, when you are confronted with this issue that's not the time to start thinking about it. It might be tempting when you're offered a great part, but this will be easier to deal with if you set your boundaries before your audition. What are your limits?

Many people have strong feelings about smoking or simulating the use of drugs. They have a difficult time playing roles that clash with their personal standards. It may be helpful to tackle this dilemma by making a list of things you simply won't do. Then make another list of things that are in that gray area.

Imagine you're caught in a fire. That's not the time to necessarily follow your instincts and run, but rather fall back on the old game plan of stop, drop and roll. Treat your career choices the same way. Being prepared may prevent you from getting burned.

---

Think through what's best for you, your career and how it will affect those closest to you.

# Chapter 27 – Learn & Utilize Technology To Your Advantage

Don't let fear hold you back from embracing technology. While it may be easier for young people who've grown up with flashing screens and hand held devices, you have to get over the mental hurdle quickly if you are to succeed in this fast-paced world.

For example, learn how to take high quality videos, edit and instantly upload them, record great sound, sharpen up your resume with multi-media, and market your product (yourself) on social media. You would be surprised how many people have not mastered the basics. They rely on outside help that can eat up time and money. This is an industry that increasingly makes it easier for the individual to be self-sufficient.

**Dan's Take**

If you're short on money, don't worry. Take advantage of the many free resources out there. Libraries, for example, offer a diverse menu of services and equipment for individuals and small businesses. Get comfortable with a host of free apps that can turn self-produced projects into professional quality work.

**Lau's Take**

Now, there's good news and bad news. The good news is that there's more power in the palm of your hand. The bad news is that expectations have risen.

What we mean by that is people who are looking for talent and hiring want your marketing materials at the drop of a hat. They may email you at 9:00 in the morning with a request to re-edit your resume, update your clips or provide them with a different headshot or voice sample by noon. They know that anything is possible with today's technology. The old excuses that the copy center was closed or an editor wasn't available simply don't fly anymore.

---

It may be daunting to warm up to technology, but this industry not only demands it, it depends on it.

# Chapter 28 – Know Your Audience

As a performer, you get the chance to showcase your talents in front of diverse audiences whether you're on camera, on a live stage or behind a microphone. The challenge is that the tastes of those viewers and listeners are constantly changing and transitioning. You need to be able to stay one step ahead to remain relevant with your audience.

**Lau's Take**

It's not about you, the performer; it's about the other, your audience. You really do have to know and understand your demographic to know exactly, not only what to say, but how to say it. That way your audience won't lose interest and will keep coming back for more. It's one of the keys to surviving in this industry long term.

**Dan's Take**

I have always found that people who stubbornly hold onto their old ways and don't care to fully understand the present have a higher rate of failure. It's a great way to cut your career short.

Pay attention to the warning signs:

Ratings plummet. Contracts aren't renewed. The roles offered to you become limited.

Some may worry that over playing to what sells will compromise their artistic integrity. That is a legitimate concern.

---

There's room for compromise, but to be most effective you should always remain authentic and be keenly aware of what the audience wants.

# Chapter 29 – Your Wardrobe Makes You

If you have ever been in the Boys Scouts or Girl Scouts you have been trained to be ready. Whether it's learning how to survive in the wild or how to look just right in your uniform it's important information that can save your life or move you up in rank.

There are some basics you can learn that will help you survive in the industry on a moments notice or like the scouts move up the ranks.

### Dan's Take

I love this one because ever since I got into this business, I have always had two basics in my wardrobe: a blue blazer and a blue shirt. No lines and no busy prints. It's universal. It's great for a photo-shoot. It works well if you are on television, reporting. To mix it up a little bit, have a number of different accessories as part of your repertoire. You want to have ties with different styles and colors. You can branch out as trends come and go, but this formula never gets old. It takes some of the pressure off last minute wardrobe decisions. And it just may prevent malfunctions.

### Lau's Take

Industry staples for women's wardrobe spans from "the little black dress" to a business casual look to jeans and fitted tops. Whether you are a performer or behind the scenes your fashion is about fit and overall presence.

You can easily dress any garment up or down with a few accessories like a scarf, belt or shoes. Throw in some nice simple earrings, but avoid ostentatious jewelry. Add a gem or jewel color – cobalt, ruby or deep emerald - and stay away from too many textures, such as a fabric that is shiny and potentially distracting.

You don't have to spend thousands of dollars on high-end labels. Just stick to classic lines and classic colors that can mix and match.

If you're still having trouble deciding what works for you and have a few extra bucks, consult a stylist. If you're trying to save money, photographers are a good resource because they understand the kinds of colors that are flattering for you. Ask questions and you may get plenty of free advice and come out looking great.

# Chapter 30 – Market Like A Monster

People who are looking to enter the industry or who have been around for a while will sometimes expect their agents and managers to do everything. Agents are an important part of your professional tool kit, but remember that you are your best marketer. Don't just relax and figure that one of your representatives have "taken care of it." In other words partner with them to you get work.

**Lau's Take**

You are your own business. You represent yourself and constantly put yourself, your product and your services out there. To reinforce the importance of this concept I often advise hanging a little sign with your name (your company) on it in a visible spot. It's a psychological technique that reminds you to be proactive in marketing your business yourself. Industry professionals who have representation can often fall into a trap of relying solely on their agent or manager to find work for them. That is one pipeline, but every time you attend a social or professional function, make a cold call, send an email, or simply step out on the street, you are marketing yourself. Don't forget that.

**Dan's Take**

Pitch yourself everywhere and anywhere. Have your resumes in hand with links to your work available for instant access. 100% of the time, you are marketing. When you are not working a job, you are working on getting work. Always be on! Always hunting. This is a huge step that will play in the success or failure of your career. Get out and network. Always carry your business cards, even to the gym and hand them out whenever you can. Make sure that you have updated materials. Your tools must be with you, all the time.

If you're looking for other creative ways to market yourself, tap into local programs often at colleges and community centers. For little or no investment, you might come away with some great ideas and strategies.

---

Marketing begets marketing. The more you invest, the better the returns. Would you rely solely on your real estate agent to find your next house? Or would you check online sites, drive around a neighborhood on a Sunday afternoon and reach out to your friends on social media to see if they know of a good property in a specific area you are interested in? Of course you would. So think of your career the same way and market like a monster.

# Chapter 31 – Discover The Power Of Preparation

If you ran into a top Hollywood producer, news director or casting agent in an airport, would you be able to give them a cogent description of yourself and your work within 30 seconds? We're not talking about marketing yourself here, it's about being prepared for THE moment and thinking on your feet.

First, remember that these professionals are all busy, are constantly meeting people and are often inundated with pitches. What can you say and do that will make that chance encounter a success?

**Dan's Take**

If I am trying to develop my pitch I use a stopwatch to practice. The idea is to jam as much useful information with a bit of flair into a few seconds. If you're prepared, you have the advantage over someone who is trying to gather their thoughts at that very moment. You want to sound spontaneous and not rehearsed even though that's exactly what you've done.

**Lau's Take**

You have to do some improvisational work here, where you have to be ready to change it up and switch it, based on the audience that is in front of you. So practice it, figure out what it is, but be willing to change it along the way as you meet your different audiences.

I make a concerted effort to look at them without freaking them out and saying how are you today? Then immediately about 80% of those people start conversations with me because they are dying for some friendly exchange that may open the door. So, you have to find out what opens the door for the other person to help you with your presentation and sometimes it is just a matter of saying one very simple thing and then listening to their response.

Like many things in life advice is pretty simple, but a lot of obvious things are often overlooked. Everyone knows they should be prepared. That's obvious right? But in the end they drop the ball. If you have the option to delay a pitch or interview because you felt ill-prepared then do it. The more prepared you are the better you will be to handle your material or whatever curve ball may be thrown your way.

# Chapter 32 – How Not To Fall Apart

What is the secret to maintaining your health, mentally, emotionally and physically in this business?

Here are some tips:

Sleep, exercise, and meditate. The icing on the protein bar is time management. Don't let the clock be your enemy. Manage your time wisely. This is an important one because often we focus so much on the work, how to get the gig and how to get in front of the right people. We tend not to put focus on our personal health and wellbeing in this high-stakes, high-pressure industry. If you fall apart you are likely to burn out early. You might be able to fake it for a while, but it tends to catch up with all of us.

**Dan's Take**

Some people will say that sleep is overrated. It is not. Studies bear this out. People who get the proper amount of rest (7 to 9 hours a night) perform better at school and work. Taking naps, as is common in other countries, is also healthy. I sometimes feel a little guilty if I sleep in or take a break in the middle of the day but when things are going crazy, that's exactly what I try to do. I also try to keep myself in shape by exercising regularly. It doesn't have to be a full-blown workout session with a trainer. It could be a short walk or a few minutes of stretching.

**Lau's Take**

I like a quiet calming, combating internal chaos, focusing and rebalancing. Candles help to create that relaxing mood.

I would say too, be very aware of who you surround yourself with. If you spend time around negative people it tends to be contagious. You're going to feel bad and then ask yourself why? Sometimes work controls your environment and it becomes difficult to divorce yourself from these negative influences.

In that case try to limit your exposure and challenge yourself to have a positive attitude.

Everyone would like to take this industry by storm and make it happen in an instant.  But maintaining longevity in this career will need a steady stream of work-life balance and downtime. It's okay to be still and not always busy in active pursuit of your goals. Calmness and quiet have an impact on the quality of your work and finding the authentic you.

# Chapter 33 – Getting An Agent Or A Manager

Movies and celebrities seem to glamorize the status of having an agent or manager. In a way you feel as if you have made it or at least you are on your way, when someone agrees to represent you. But hang on just a moment. Before you make the leap you should weigh the pros and cons of representation and do the math. You may find that it makes sense on paper, but that added expense may cut into your bottom line.

**Dan's Take**

I've had an agent for the better part of my professional life. Recently, I dropped my longtime broadcast news agent and signed with someone who represents me across the entertainment field. He's constantly working with me to find the right roles and opportunities. And avoid the pitfalls that could damage my career long term, such as the infamous casting couch and whether or not I should take my clothes off.

Lau: (laugh) In New England you won't have that problem.

Dan: (laugh) It's too cold.

Agents can help you navigate some of the controversial waters that you may encounter throughout your career. They can help form a plan and lay out the right strategy to achieve your professional goals. And when it comes to difficult negotiations, or problems with management, it's great to have a good cop- bad cop dynamic

**Lau's Take**

Your agent can be your partner in action, your best friend and at the very least, your close colleague.  The bottom line is, they are working for you but the goal is to make money for both of you. You want to be sure that the relationship is a good fit and that the kind of work they are submitting you for is not only what you desire but what will further your career. Eventually you may need multiple agents depending on whether you are signed exclusively with an agency or are freelancing.

Getting a manager might also make sense. They get paid to keep track of the big picture and are there to advise you when your career gets more complex and you have multiple options with money at stake.

It's not a given that you can get representation right off the bat. There's a dance that goes on. You have to show promise before they'll take interest. And once you are in, that doesn't guarantee that you'll stay. Agencies routinely have a one-year trial period. If you aren't getting booked then they are less inclined to keep you around but remember they work for you.

Some people like to go with the "big name" agencies if they are offered the chance, because they feel that it would be more prestigious and that it comes with more firepower and connections. The downside is that you may get lost in the shuffle and not receive the personal attention that you expected unless you rise to A-list level.

---

There's another route to take and that is to go with a smaller more personalized agency that may give you a lot of attention. Boutiques may increase your chances of getting steady work because there's less in-house competition.

These tips can be helpful early on as you're getting started or as you seek to reboot your career. Representation can help you get there if it's the right fit.

# Chapter 34 – Be Nice Always

In an industry where tempers run high and people with big egos deliver low blows, being nice is not only the right thing to do, it's a valuable asset. You don't have to be nice to be successful, but it helps in many ways. It takes some of the tension out of the air and makes for a better working environment. It might come back to help you. People don't forget nice.

**Dan's Take**

While nice folks don't always finish first, people tend to remember those who have taken the time and effort to be respectful and courteous.

There was a reporter I worked with many years ago who asked for some professional pointers. In this competitive atmosphere, some of my other colleagues would have balked at giving him advice. But I helped him. Flash forward 20 years. That reporter is now a news manager who reached out to me, and reminded me of the time I took to help him out. He was in a position now to return the favor and offered me several opportunities.

**Lau's Take**

Not to sound too Pollyanna-like, but the truth is that when you are nice and you are doing for others -those random acts of kindness as the bumper sticker says - you become a better person. When you're more thoughtful you're happier.  Of course, not everything is going to work out, but when your true character shines through it's easier to take the hits gracefully and people take notice.

Dan:  I have never forgotten people who have been nice to me along the way.

Lau: Isn't that amazing. It's quite an asset. You can go further sometimes by just being nice.

Dan:  That is right, so to sum it up, be nice to someone, no matter where they stand in the office. They could open doors for you. Being nice is not only good; it's good for business.

Lau: It is also good for your complexion and good for your health. (Laugh)

Dan:  That's right, like drinking water. (Laugh)

---

When directors, producers, crews, talent and others in the industry are nice it tends to take some of the tension out of the air and results in a better working environment. That could result in a much better product or, at the very least, create a different narrative for the tabloids to write about. After all, nice would be the breaking news. No?

# Chapter 35 – Get A Qualified Coaching Team

When you are struggling to make it in the business or thinking about getting started, the last thing you want to do is spend more money on other things. Think of this chapter as an investment not as a frivolous impulse purchase.

**Lau's Take**

I've been coaching for more years than I'd like to admit and can attest to the benefits of an experienced and qualified coaching team. Why would you try to cut corners with your career? After all, you may be willing to pay for a trainer to get physically fit or a financial advisor to handle your money, or other ventures that may benefit your lifestyle why not your career?

We call it learning money. Reputable coaches can save you from disappointment and help figure out an action plan to hone your craft. Even people who are at the top of their game require regular coaching. What I'm talking about is a personalized program. Not in a group, not a class dynamic, but paying specific attention to areas that need improvement or adjusting as well as celebrating what is successful and working well.

**Dan's Take**

A Do It Yourself Project, DIY is good when you are working around the house, but it doesn't always translate to your career. A coaching team - much like in sports - keeps you committed and makes you responsible. It keeps you in training. It gives you a sense of security. It's the role of a trusted advisor to help strengthen your career.

---

Finally, it is also about accountability in an industry where it is very easy to become distracted, fall off the wagon, so to speak and lose your way. A coach can help you stay on track.

# Chapter 36 – Be the Fixer Upper

Everything we do in life is about identifying the problem and fixing it. This industry is no different. There is constantly a need whether it's behind the scenes or in front of the camera. Sometimes the producer's or employer's number one choice backs out of a project at the last minute and they need someone to step in immediately. Wouldn't it be nice if you were to be the one to fill that need? Often the opportunities go to those who are not only flexible, but prepared and ready to jump in.

**Lau's Take**

Put yourself in the position of a casting director whose back is up against the wall because two lead performers have dropped out. One was sick the other had a family issue. The perfect person for the job is often the one right in front of them who says yes, I can make it to that location in a half hour. Time is always of the essence.

**Dan' Take:**

When I was looking for my first job I visited a television station and asked if there were any openings. There were none. Yet I left my resume, sold my talents and abilities and prayed that I had left a good impression. The next week I received a phone call from the news director with a job offer. "Can you start right away?" I said yes. It turns out I was the fixer upper even though I didn't realize it at the time. There had been a sudden departure of one of their reporters. My resume and offer to be available immediately sealed the deal.

---

In a hyper aggressive industry, you have to look for ways to gain an edge. Being there and ready to go can cut out a tremendous amount of competition.

# Chapter 37 – Visualize Your Destiny

If you think you are not going to succeed, if you have doubts, then you probably won't succeed. Imagine where you want to go, paint a clear picture of that scene in your mind, act as if it is happening. That's the power of visualization.

**Lau Take**

So, mindset is one of the most powerful tools that you possess. You must learn to manage it and strategize, plot and plan. It is very important that you don't forget that you are the one in charge of setting your own mindset, meaning that the tone that you are bringing into the room, into the audition, into the interview is the tone that is going to be picked up by the person on the other side of the desk. It will help them evaluate if you are the right person for the job. It all happens in a flash.

**Dan's Take**

My young daughter is a sprinter and she has done quite well for her age. One of the things that she likes to do when she's at the start line is to visualize that she is going to win. There is no doubt about it in her mind. And you know what, she often does win. Her motto is quite simple: "If I didn't visualize a win then why go out there in the first place."

It doesn't mean that the mindset that you have will always be equal to the result, but if you keep walking up to the start line thinking "I am never going to get that job," then you know what? Your doubts will play out in real life. So, when you are waiting for that gun to fire off, imagine that you are going to win every single time.

---

In this rat race where one is constantly going from gig to gig, rejection is par for the course. With that in mind many people come to expect failure. It turns into a self-fulfilling prophecy after a while. Is your mindset responsible for your success? Well to some degree yes, it probably is.

# Chapter 38 – Don't Quit Your Day Job

Before you take the leap to follow your dreams make sure you have a financial safety net. Set aside enough money to cover your expenses for a period of six months to a year. Why?

## Lau's Take

We operate in an uncertain environment. Getting a major deal in radio, television, film or any other multi-media platforms doesn't guarantee that the money train will keep rolling. After a certain amount of time, that contract is going to end and you might not get work for months if not years. Those who make it over the long term are the ones who understand this concept well.

It might be helpful to take some small steps. For example, in addition to your day job, cast a wide net for opportunities within the industry. See what sticks. Are you able to get good roles? Would it be consistent work? Are your technical skills in high demand? If you answered yes to all those questions then you are probably are one step closer to your end goal.

## Dan's Take

I know of someone who got a really great role and then decided at that point, this is going to lead to a better role and a much better role and a much better role after that. They quit their day job and unfortunately that was the last big role they got. So, after their money ran out they had to start looking for another day job, if you will. Thinking this through more carefully could have prevented some of the heartache and stress.

---

Look in to the future before you launch into something new in the present so that you know how to take care of yourself and your family.

# Chapter 39 – Learn To Work Really, Really, Really Hard

Flying into Hollywood on a Friday afternoon and hitting the jackpot by Monday with a starring role or screenwriting credit does happen, but it is highly unlikely. What typically goes on behind the scenes is a lot of hard work. Hours and years of tryouts, lessons, smaller projects, mailroom jobs, etc. are what lead to those perceived instant successes.

### Lau's Take

It's all about understanding and respecting the process and not signing up merely for fame and fortune.

So many people come into my studio looking for voice over roles, acting and modeling jobs, and coaching. I can't tell you how many of them seriously thought they were going to be an overnight success. In another chapter (Chapter 37), we discussed how important it is to visualize winning. We don't want to undo that, but there's a certain stark reality. There's a wide gap between the number of people who become stars and the number of people who don't make it.

But don't despair. If you're willing to work hard and sacrifice there are plenty of opportunities to make a career out of your passion even if you don't always get top billing.

### Dan's Take

You brought up a good point because when people see someone who came out of nowhere and they are labeled as "overnight successes" what they don't see is that those people were selling albums out of the back of a car in a parking lot, working in community theater, or riding up and down the elevator waiting to give cold copy and slip a resume to someone in power. Don't be duped by that notion. If it happens to you, that's great, you are lucky, you won the lottery.

Are you ready to put in the kind of work necessary to make this a successful career? This is a 24/7 industry. You might be on location for months on end or may have to rehearse nightly for an extended amount of time or work at odd hours. It's a grind that pays dividends in satisfaction, a decent living and for a few rocket ship successes.

# Chapter 40 – Have A Sense of Humor

Taking your job seriously is important, but that doesn't mean you can't have fun. There is no need to be so serious about everything that is happening so that you lose your natural sense of fun and humor. That is a universal connection with people, especially in our industry. We love to have fun. Don't lose it, because that is going to get you through the stress, the long hours and the disappointments.

**Dan's Take**

When I was starting out at one of my early jobs, we weren't being paid much. What really carried us through those moments were the times when we could all laugh at our circumstances together. We couldn't believe how silly it was that we were holding things together with tape and glue. I remember some of our tape deck machines were always broken and you had to remove the lid to stick your hand in there and spin a gear or do something, to get it working again. It was so ridiculous that the humor was what kept us going at the time. It certainly wasn't the pay. Keep a good sense of humor and a smile on your face even during challenging times.

**Lau's Take**

Having recognized the importance of humor in the workplace you still have to be careful about when and where it's appropriate. Depending on what kind of humor it is, it could potentially be inappropriate or non-PC. Or you may be too new to the job or project for people to "get" you and that could lead to uncomfortable situations. Sometimes the camaraderie takes time to develop.

I've had colleagues with no sense of humor, and during phone conversations my jokes are met with silence. They have no idea that you even cracked a joke. So, you have to listen very carefully and follow along as you gauge what kind of humor or lack thereof your personal audience has.

Take the time to laugh at yourself and at some of the madness that goes with the territory. Humor can brighten things on a stressful set. It may help take some of the fear out of the moment, and according to doctors it helps with memory, boosts your immune system and fight heart disease. Now that's no joke.

# Chapter 41 – Leaping Over Hurdles

There are several ways to view a hurdle in your path. You can be prepared, leap and stay focused on the course ahead. You can stop, sit and worry over how to move forward. Or you can take an awkward jump, get your foot caught and fall flat on your face. Which of those examples speaks to you? What would you like it to be?

## Dan's Take

One of my companies got a great opportunity to take on a major production. It required heavy lifting and corralling many moving parts. We were faced with some difficult hurdles. Guests we had booked began to cancel. A camera stopped working and graphics we had prepared had to be changed at the last minute. At one point, I felt like the example above, of sitting down and surrendering because it all felt too difficult to overcome. But I didn't do that. Why? I've always anticipated hurdles. That allowed me to pull from Plan B and even Plan C to finally clear the hurdle and sneak the production in right under the deadline.

## Lau's Take

One big hurdle that I see is that actors and other performers who come to the table with physical and emotional disabilities. Whether it's autism or someone who is visually impaired there are huge challenges that can be overcome, but that can also stand in the way of success. Some of my clients find that they have to pull over and come up with strategies to leap over their hurdles. Others give up. But there are those who come into the industry with realistic expectations and a strategy to jump over barriers that would trip others up. It often means working twice as hard to anticipate not only the usual potholes in the road, but how they might also impact their disabilities. What's amazing is the tenacity and optimism that they often have. It's more than proving they can make it in the business, it's showing the industry their disability doesn't make them any less capable of clearing everyday hurdles.

---

Make a list of any foreseeable hurdles in your career. Talk to people who've "been there" or enlist the help of a coach. Research how others have handled hurdles and be inspired.

# Chapter 42 – Turn Your Competitor Into Your Colleague

In every industry, there's competition. For some that's a scary concept. It means someone else is in your space threatening your pathway to success. In this business, some would argue that the competitive knives are even sharper. So, what can you do about it?

**Dan's Take**

I would suggest taking the opportunity to study the people who are competing with you. Watch, learn, and do. This may help you to get a leg up, getting an edge from your competition.  They may even reveal important tips.

**Lau's Take**

Keep in mind that your competitors have different mindsets. There are many competitors, and, get ready for this, who do not play nice in the sandbox. They do not want to share their toys and their space. Even then, there's still a lot you can pick up from them whether they're willing to share anything or not. Being around healthy competition can strengthen you as a professional.

---

Another tip to beat the competition is to be different. Allow the energy to feed your creativity, which in turn may help you to stand out. Become known as a non-complainer and gain a reputation as being easy to work with. You might even consider turning to humor, if appropriate, to separate yourself from the pack. And finally, use thank you notes as a follow-up to your audition or job interview. That is becoming a lost art, but it's still appreciated.

# Chapter 43 – Surround Yourself With People Who Are More Seasoned & Experienced

Want to get better at your game without going back to school? Try surrounding yourself with people who are more seasoned and experienced than you. It's always been said that if you're playing a sport against a better opponent your game improves.

**Dan's Take**

On the flip side, stay away from the negative forces that could destroy or heavily damage your confidence and professional outlook. Whiners, complainers and people who tend to give up easily aren't the best company for you.

**Lau's Take**

This sphere that you create around you is really a sphere of energy and vibes that will work to your advantage. If you surround yourself with greatness, people are going to automatically be attracted to your circle. They might also associate your name with success.

You always want to be authentic in your personal and professional lives. The people close to you should matter not because of what they do, but who they are. However, when it comes to professional matters it's wise to consider these strategies.

---

Just remember you are merely a spoke in the wheel of a community who has been doing their jobs for many years. Their job is to make you look great. So make their jobs as easy as possible.

# Chapter 44 – Don't Take The Easy Road

It's been often said, "The easy roads are crowded." What that means is that most people take the path of least resistance. They are searching for shortcuts to overnight success. They do as little as possible and bristle at hurdles and challenges. There's much to be said for taking the difficult path. It can build character and strengthen your craft leading to a more successful and rewarding career.

## Lau's Take

I always say, when you are making choices, the bigger the mountain the richer the experience. When you are presented with roles or other opportunities that stretch your skills you are going to think a little deeper. You are going to be a little bit more layered and sophisticated about the way you present what you are doing. It may also motivate you to explore new avenues that will result in a more compelling and interesting performances.

## Dan's Take

When I help my kids with their math homework I've learned that the teachers don't want to just see the final answer. They want to see the formula, how you got there. It's a longer and often more difficult process to reach the same conclusion. But it builds a better and deeper understanding of math. Likewise, working your way through a more difficult formula in the industry can have the same results. When I just started working at my first reporter job in a small market, I received a better offer from another company. It meant more money, better hours, more visibility and more sophisticated tools that would make my job easier. I ended up taking a pass on that opportunity so that I could grind it out and learn from my mistakes before moving on up. I credit that decision with preparing me for a much bigger career.

---

So, don't be afraid of the more challenging pathway. It may take a little longer and be a little more jarring, but that's how backbones are formed and careers are weatherproofed.

# Chapter 45 – Follow Up

Following up to a meeting, interview or audition is essential to advancing your career. Too many times people expect an answer back and don't initiate any contact, and that would be called "resting on your laurels." We call that careless and possibly lazy.

**Dan's Take**

I like to send out periodic emails. Keeping myself in the line of vision even though there's no new development is a good strategy to stand out from the pack. Every major holiday and every few months I do check-ins with contacts. I go through my email list and send out greetings and/or news.

It's a short and sweet reminder. "I just want to let you know that I'm around and available."

I also find that people in the industry appreciate handwritten notes more than you would think, because nobody seems to do that anymore. It's an outdated tradition that personalizes your communication, and a friendly way of keeping in touch.

Many people will follow up with one quick email and that's it. What they don't realize is that email could have been lost in the shuffle or may be floating around in cyberspace! That's a reason why routinely reaching out is important.

Some of you might worry that too much of this will be annoying and you'll be labeled a nuisance. What's important here is for you to find the right balance between nagging and following up. Some of you may think you have nothing going on, to share. But you always have something going on. It could be coaching, a performance, a class or working on your demos. Find something in there to show that you are staying active in the business, and it doesn't necessarily mean that it's a paid job.

You can also use these virtual check-ins to initiate meetings and other opportunities. It's more than saying thank you. It's a subtle way to say let's do business together.

**Lau's Take**

Many performers are super talented and have a ton to offer, but can be intimidated by the simple process of staying in touch.

I have a client who came in recently and told me that she was so afraid to follow up with a panel for which she had recently auditioned so she let it go.

She's very talented and told me she never knew what to say in a follow-up email. She felt that sending periodic emails borders is stalking. I said, just let them know that you are still interested in the role and in any other projects they may have down the road. Don't worry about what they might think. The worse they can do is ignore you. Keep after them and stay top of mind.

---

The biggest problem is talent not following up. It's a big issue. Mark your calendar to remind yourself of the people you should stay in touch with. Sometimes just the timing of your email could land you a great opportunity, because at that moment your face or your resume is just what they're looking for.

It's important to stay on the radar and conquer that irrational fear of being a bother.

# Chapter 46 – Stay On Top of Your Industry

Expose yourself to radio, TV, music, social media and whatever other new platforms, so you can be up to date with the jobs that are out there now. Follow the trends. It will keep you on top of your game.

**Lau's Take**

Be aware. Be awake. Don't put yourself to sleep. Know what is going on in the medium that you want to work in. If you want to be in television or be a producer, great! You have to follow your favorite producers and watch their shows. You have to know what kind of work schedule they are keeping. Be familiar with their networks and watch all their projects.

This all helps you to be aware of what is happening in your industry today, what people are talking about and what they care about.

**Dan's Take**

Here's a couple of examples: You have an interview where they ask, "Hey, what did you think of our film that premiered this weekend?" Or "What's your take on the merger of these two big film studios?" If you didn't do your homework you're caught off guard and you don't know what to say. This could put you at a disadvantage for being hired, because you might be viewed as someone who isn't interested enough to care about current activity in the business. It reflects negatively on your work ethic.

---

That's why you have to stay plugged-in. At the same time, be careful of getting overwhelmed, stressed out, or panic stricken because you don't know everything that's going on and can't keep up with every conversation about every medium. A basic knowledge is better than being clueless and out of the loop.

# Chapter 47 – Organize Your Way to Success

Being organized may lead to success. But like the foundation of your house, organization needs to be the foundation of your career. What we mean by that is putting things in order will help not only your mindset, but your focus. Establishing your uncluttered space will help you tackle your priorities and get it done.

**Dan's Take**

For me, a physical office space works very well. It helps me to be organized and keeps me from getting distracted. It doesn't have to be a professional space in a class A office building or studio. It can be a dedicated corner in your basement, bedroom, or walk-in closet. Every time you enter that space it puts you in a business frame of mind. I found that working out of a spare bedroom made me more productive. I didn't have to spend my day running around trying to find things and wasting my valuable time. When I created that space my profits, benefits and job opportunities increased.

**Lau's Take**

I'm a big fan of physical space. It doesn't have to be big. It doesn't have to be expensive and it doesn't have to be fancy. It just has to be your space. It has to have your name there. Make the space yours, whether it is your audio studio, whether it is a desk where you are going to be writing, whether it is your marketing nook. Sometimes it is your psychological space. That is powerful.

Being organized will also create the mental space to be more creative, to be inspired. You might even find an old business card, photograph or restaurant napkin that triggers your next deal.

---

Organization is essential and key to your success. Everything from space, time management and prioritizing tasks are necessary for accomplishing your short and long term goals.

# Chapter 48 – Diversify Your Career

Opening your mind and widening your orbit to include different people, places and perspectives is not only a wise personal goal, but good for business.

A diverse view of the world and perhaps a new language and culture along the way gives you a richer vault from which to draw upon for acting roles or journalist endeavors.

## Dan's Take

I've found that my news reports involving people of different cultures have been enhanced by diverse opportunities including travel to more than 50 countries. It gives you context. It can also impact relationships in the workplace. Knowing people of other cultures, ethnicities and religious beliefs will make you better suited for working in this industry. Learning one or several other languages also makes you more marketable. An authentic accent typically outperforms someone who is well rehearsed.

## Lau's Take

I think diversity in our industry is the name of the game. Being able to acclimate and assimilate very quickly with people who are very different from you is priceless.  There's a certain joy, energy, connection and collaboration. It is bound to inform your work. It is going to inform the kind of person you are and the kind of work you do. Let's say you are a writer. You are going to have a global mindset. You will have some ideas that may not have been sparked by just sitting in your living room.

---

This diversity push may force you out of your comfort zone. It may not come naturally to you, but it's well worth the time and investment.  You never know what will happen when you open yourself to the world and it becomes part of you.

# Chapter 49 – Empathy is Good

Empathy is a magical word. If you lack empathy, you lack an awful lot. It's a deep understanding and sense of what someone else is going through and is feeling.

Why is this important?

**Lau's Take**

As an actor, you must have that. It's can be an essential component of completing a successful performance. There is an empowering psychological effect that can take place when someone feels like you truly care about them. It could be between actors or a real-life character you are seeking to portray. Empathy helps to build trust must quicker.

**Dan's Take**

I love the show "Undercover Boss." I know it's reality TV, but there is always that time in the show when the boss drives audiences and contestants to tears with deep empathy. A mortgage gets paid off, hospital bills for an ailing relative are taken care of, or a much-needed raise changes a struggling families' life. That display of empathy tugs at my heart and wins points for the boss and their company.

---

Whether you're on a set or in a newsroom, connecting on a heart level can have positive consequences. You shouldn't force it, but be open to expressing it. Listen when people speak. Make them feel enriched, make them feel empowered; make them feel like you truly cared then see what happens.

# Chapter 50 – Don't Live in the Past, Succeed in the Present

History is very important. Looking in the rearview mirror can't keep you from repeating the same mistakes, over and over again, in life and in your career. But spending too much time selling yourself on what you have done in the distant past doesn't work if you aren't burnishing your portfolio in the present.

**Lau's Take**

You have to be relevant by working, working, working. Even if it's a small role or a freelance news job, everything you do now will add more muscle to what you have done in the past. At some point, you have to drop the credits from high school or community theatre. They might be important at the start, but not when you are 47 years old. (Believe me people do this all the time) Stay relevant, very contemporary and very fresh.

**Dan's Take**

I like to say, "Add one, subtract one." What I mean by that is every time you get a bigger role or new opportunity, look to shave those earlier experiences off your resume. Now, if you were the child star on a movie that was the highest grossing film ever, then shout it from the mountaintops for your entire career. However, even that can't define you at 47 if there's very little else. So, use the past to give some context to everything that you have done, but don't rely too heavily on things that have clearly surpassed the expiration date.

---

If you are struggling to come up with significant current roles, then find ways to take what's old and make it new. Repackage old videos into new webisodes that you post on YouTube. Stitch together clips into a fresh documentary. Take dated articles from the vault and use them to inspire new materials. This puts you in the driver's seat, clearly looking out the front windshield instead of the rearview mirror.

And launches you on the road to MEGA CRUSH YOUR MEDIA CAREER.

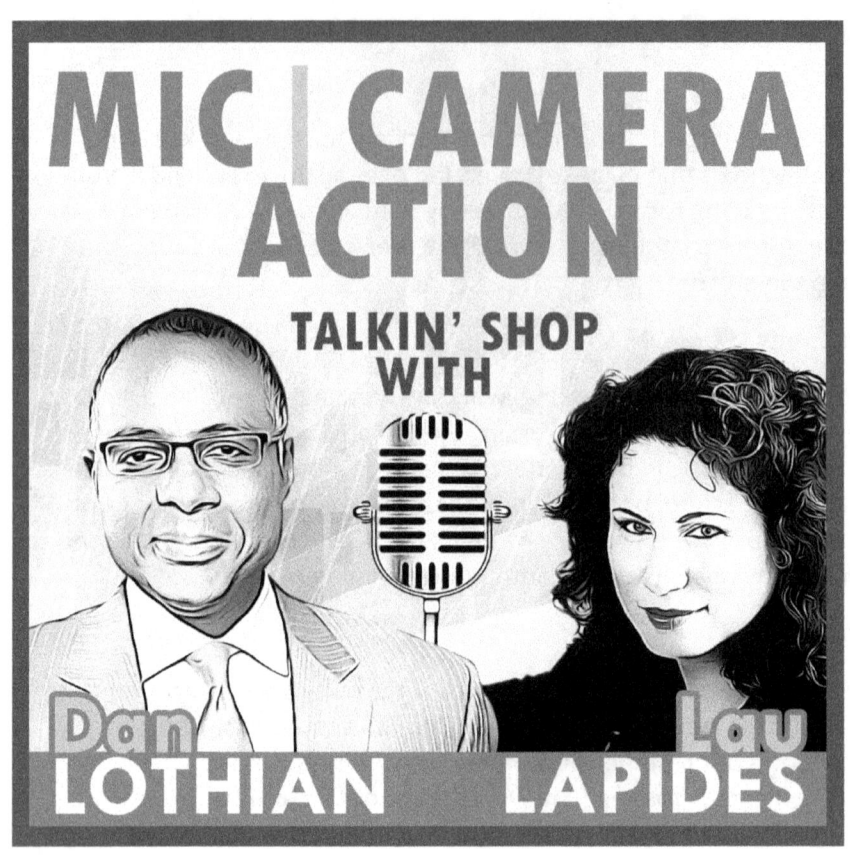

Listen to our podcast, *Mic, Camera, Action: Talkin' Shop With Dan Lothian and Lau Lapides* located on CLNS Media Podcast Network, Speak Up Talk Radio Network, iTunes, Stitcher and laulapidescompany.com

www.ingramcontent.com/pod-product-compliance
Lightning Source LLC
Chambersburg PA
CBHW070110210526
45170CB00013B/808